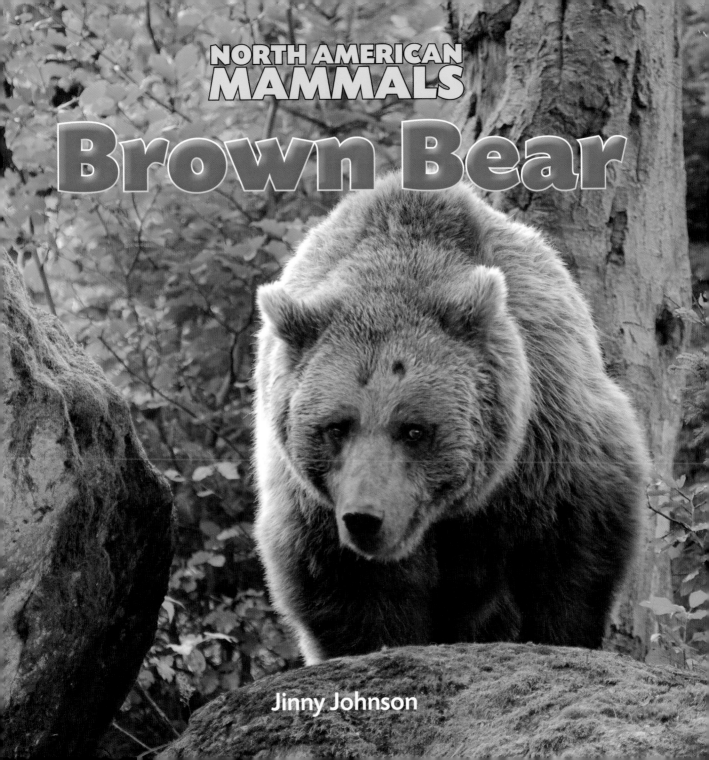

NORTH AMERICAN MAMMALS
Brown Bear

Jinny Johnson

Published by Smart Apple Media,
an imprint of Black Rabbit Books
P.O. Box 3263, Mankato, Minnesota, 56002
www.blackrabbitbooks.com

Printed in the United States of America,
at Corporate Graphics in North Mankato, Minnesota.

Designed by Hel James
Edited by Mary-Jane Wilkins

Cataloging-in-Publication Data
is available from the Library of Congress

ISBN 978-1-62588-032-1

Photo acknowledgements
t = top, b = bottom
title page Stefan Simmerl/Shutterstock; page 3 BMJ/
Shutterstock; 4 Tony Campbell, 5 Dan Kosmayer/both
Shutterstock; 6 iStockphoto/Thinkstock; 7 Erik Mandre/
Shutterstock; 8 un.bolovan/Shutterstock; 9 iStockphoto/
Thinkstock; 10 NancyS, 11 Kane513/both Shutterstock;
12 BGSmith/Shutterstock; 13 iStockphoto/Thinkstock;
14 iliuta goean, 15 Erik Mandre/both Shutterstock;
16, 17 Galyna Andrushko/Shutterstock; 18, 19, 20 iStockphoto/
Thinkstock, 22t Ewan Chesser, b basel101658/both Shutterstock;
23 iStockphoto/Thinkstock
Cover Randy Yarbrough/Shutterstock

DAD0509
052013
9 8 7 6 5 4 3 2 1

Contents

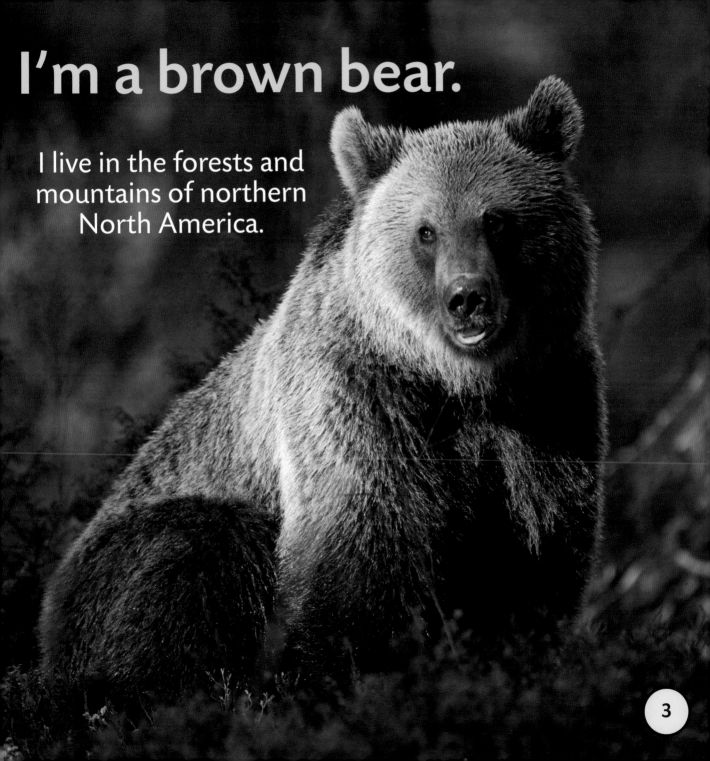

I'm a brown bear.

I live in the forests and mountains of northern North America.

First Weeks

My sisters and I were born in our mother's warm den in the middle of winter.

4

We were tiny and helpless, but our mom kept us safe. She fed us with her milk for our first few months and we grew quickly.

Fun Outdoors

In the spring we started to come out of our den and explore— but always with mom nearby.

My sisters and I had lots of fun chasing each other and having wrestling matches.

We liked to try to catch insects and other small creatures. It was good practice for hunting.

Big Bear

We think our mom is cuddly, but she is really strong and can be fierce.

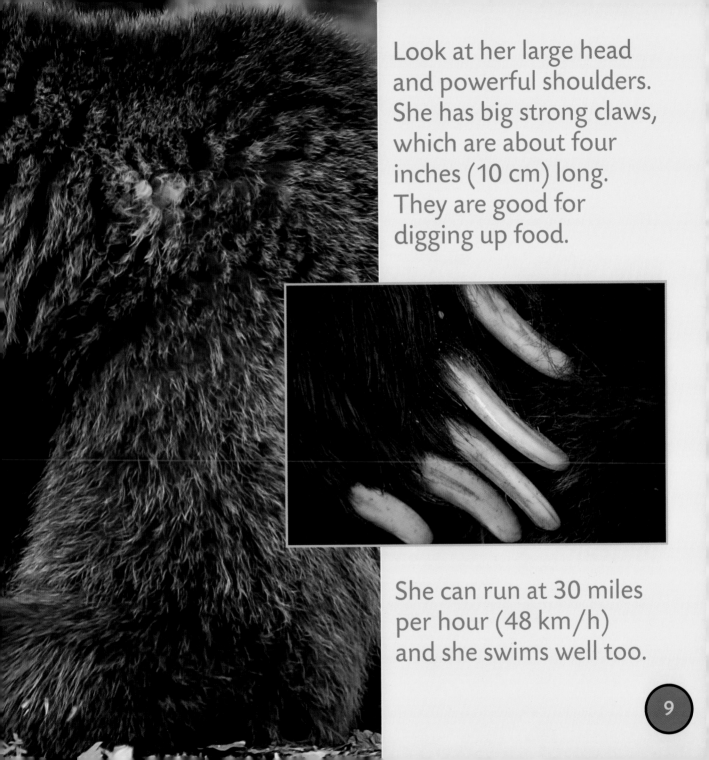

Look at her large head and powerful shoulders. She has big strong claws, which are about four inches (10 cm) long. They are good for digging up food.

She can run at 30 miles per hour (48 km/h) and she swims well too.

Keeping Warm

Our very thick fur keeps us warm, but we shed some in summer, when it's hot.

We're called brown bears, but we're not all the same color. Some are very light brown and others are almost black.

Other brown bears have silvery-white tips on the hairs and these bears are known as "grizzlies."

Favorite Foods

Brown bears eat lots of different foods. Much of the time we feed on nuts, berries, leaves, and roots.

We watch our mom closely to see what she eats. That's how we learn to find food for ourselves.

Big bears like my mom hunt animals such as mice, rats, and squirrels. She can even attack moose and other big creatures.

Bear Senses

Brown bears can see and hear well,
but it's our nose that is most important.
Our sense of smell is better than a dog's.

Smell helps us find food. We also use smell to check out who has passed nearby and we leave scent marks to tell other bears that we're around.

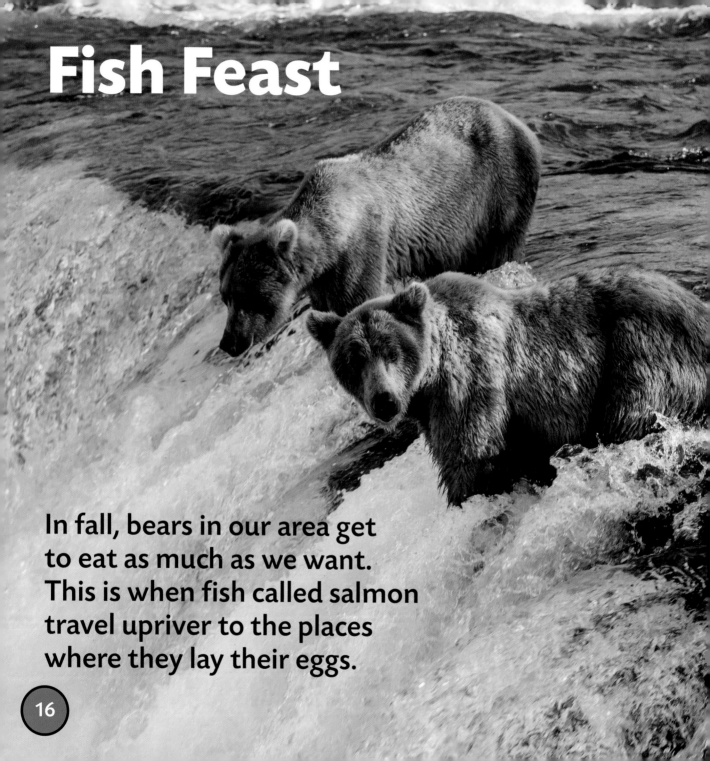

Fish Feast

In fall, bears in our area get to eat as much as we want. This is when fish called salmon travel upriver to the places where they lay their eggs.

We plunge into the water and catch lots of fish—at least my mom does. I watch her carefully, but I'm not very good at fishing yet.

17

Ready for Winter

It's important to eat lots in summer and fall so we get big and fat. This keeps us going in winter, when there is very little food around.

Most bears hide away and
sleep for much of the winter.
We get ready by digging
a den in a sheltered hillside.

This den has an entrance and
a tunnel leading to a space
where we sleep. We drag
in plants to sleep on.

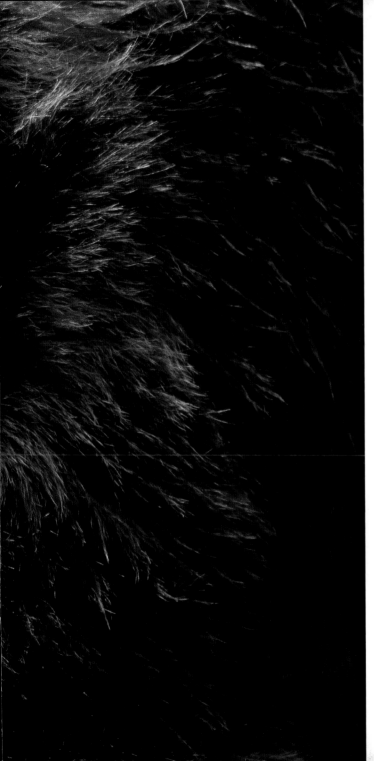

Winter Sleep

Once winter comes, we settle down in our den.

We don't eat anything at all during this time. We don't even go pee or poop. We do wake up from time to time and have a stretch.

By the time spring comes we will be over a year old, but we'll still have lots to learn.

21

Brown Bear Facts

A male brown bear weighs 300-850 pounds (136-385 kg)—five times as much as an average person. Females weigh 200-450 pounds (90-204 kg). An average brown bear is about 6 feet (1.8 m) long, with a small tail, although some are bigger.

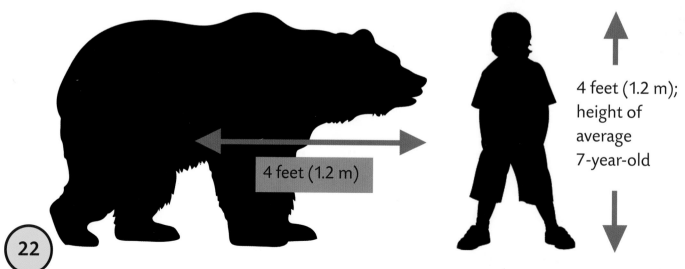

4 feet (1.2 m)

4 feet (1.2 m); height of average 7-year-old

Brown bears also live in northern Europe and Asia. In fact, brown bears live over a larger area of the world than any other kind of bear.

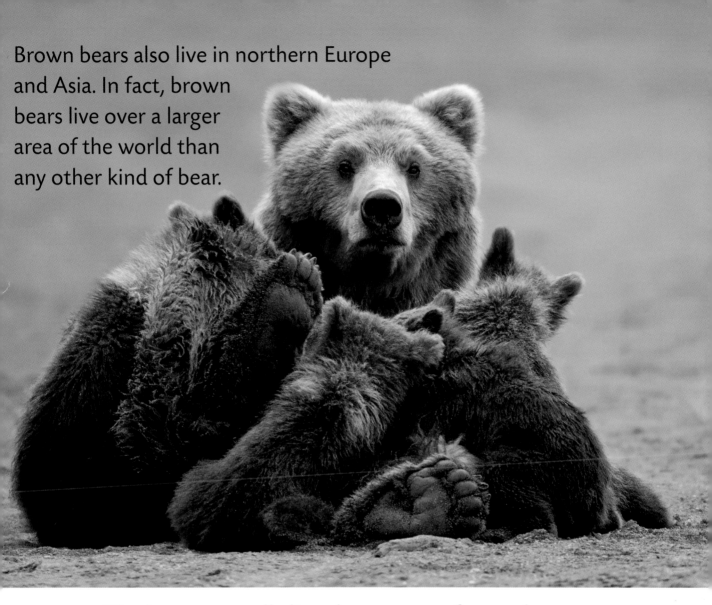

The bears generally live alone, except for mothers with cubs. The young stay with their mother for up to three years. Groups of bears gather where there is lots of food, such as rivers full of salmon.

Useful Words

den The home of an animal such as a bear.
A den is usually underground.

salmon A type of fish that spends some of its life
in the sea, but swims into rivers to mate and lay eggs.

shed When an animal sheds hair, some hair
falls out so the coat is less thick.

Index

Web Link

Learn more about brown bears at
www.sandiegozoo.org/animalbytes/t-brown_bear